Information bits and tips

for Competitive Intelligence

Henri Dou

douhenri@yahoo.fr

Henri Dou, Engineer, did his doctorate in the field of Organic Chemistry partly in Canada. After a career at the CNRS as Research Director, he joined the University of Aix Marseilles as Professor of Information Science and he developed the first French cursus in Technology Watch as well as various diplomas DU, DESS, DEA, Master, PhD in the field of Competitive Technical Intelligence, Regional Development, Bibliometrics, Strategic Development and innovation. He participated to the development of Competitive Intelligence in Brazil. He was during his career General Secretary of ChIN (Chemical Information Network UNESCO), Scientific Secretary near the General Manager of the CNRS for the cooperation CNRS-MIT (Science and Decision), "Chargé de mission" near the Manager of the Chemical sector of the CNRS for the co-operation with Rhône-Poulenc, French representative at the International Oceanographic Commission and in charge for the CNRS of the analysis of the US coal plan development and Director of a NATO advanced Institute.

He is today consultant for the World Bank, the WIPO, the OAPI and the EU, President of the French Society of Applied Bibliometrics, External Member of the CESER (Conseil Economique Social et Environnemental PACA), Director of the CIWORLDWIDE think tank and Manager of the Matheo Software company. He is also a Member of various editorial boards of scientific journals. He is specialized in Competitive Intelligence, APA (Automatic Patent Analysis), Regional Development and SRR (Social Research Responsibility). He currently takes part in various activities in Indonesia, China, Malaysia, Brazil, Africa and Mexico. More information is available on http://www.ciworldwide.org

4

Table of Content

Part 1 : The « Google World »

In Competitive Intelligence it is necessary to bypass the information overload to create competitive advantage. Overcoming the "information obesity" is important since it will allow you to focus your attention on the useful information. The information technology progress allows the development of many different information sources (even is the production of information is more or less accurate or if it is the repetition of existing one). The problem of information retrieval is that if it is well taught in documentation schools or in information science and documentation, it not the case in the other disciplines and this is a problem. The facilities offered by Internet are easily available to everyone, but their use is not optimal for the greater part of them. In this chapter we will present some basic techniques which will provide a base from which information retrieval will be easier and better. We will focus mainly on the free access source and products or on the low cost one. This book does not deal with bibliometrics and information analysis with specific software. For more information about these technics, consult the books: Automatic Patent Analysis[1] and The Diagonal of Risks - Examples from APA and Medline[2].

---

[1] Henri Dou, Automatic Patent Analysis. Example, Kindle format, Amazon, 2015
https://www.amazon.fr/Automatic-Patent-Analysis-Examples-English-ebook/dp/B010DBEWJ0/ref=asap_bc?ie=UTF8
[2] Henri Dou, The diagonal od risks. Examples from APA and Medline, Editions Universitaires Eropéennes, 2016 ISBN 978-3-8416-1466-7

1 - Google in advanced mode

When we speak of the Google's world we means all the tools and information sources offer by Google. We do not want to open a debate on the hegemony of Google but as it responds to our needs we will use it preferentially.

If most of the people use Google by writing a few words in the Google windows and perform their search it should be note:

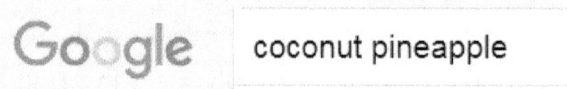

Figure 1 The implicit AND operator

- That we will retrieve all URLs which contains the words coconut AND pineapple. So implicitly is the Boolean operator AND which is used.
- The number of answers obtained are very large and we cannot make the difference between the URL containing **coconut NOT pineapple** neither the URL containing **coconut OR pineapple**. The NOT and OR are two other Boolean operators. How to access to these two operators? This must be done through the expert mode of Google.

The following figures give the process to access to Google expert (or advanced) mode. This mode is available in different language, since Google direct you on the language of the country were you are using Google. If you want to use to Google US (which is personally what I am doing) when you open Google go to the bottom right of the screen and select Google.com

Figure 2 Getting advanced mode

To ge to advanced mode go on the top right of the screen, click on he black crown and select "advanced search".

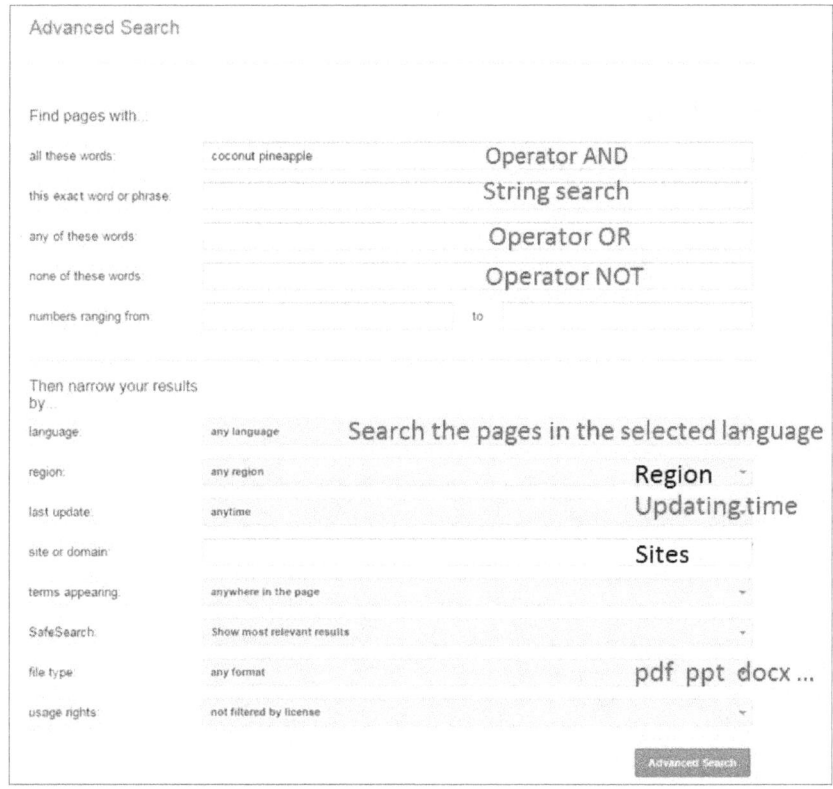

Figure 3 Advanced search mode

The most useful search tips are indicated in RED and the less useful in BLACK.

The string search mode means the retrieval of the part of a phrase, a chemical name for instance as it is written in the window.

Note that all the words are put automatically in quote. You can do the same without using the advanced search screen, you will save time!

2 - Google Scholar

When you use Google itself, you will get all he URL without distinction. But, for academics and researchers, this introduces a lot of noise and most of the results published in scientific journals are not available. To provide this information, Google has developed a specific Google: Google Scholar. Google Scholar makes available most of the scientific literature and its coverage is most important than Scopus or the Web of Science because its index also various journals, reports and papers which are not present in the "classical" databases. It also gets data from Open access journals. Then Google Scholar is very interesting when you are looking for a wide range of papers giving a good overview of a domain or an application or a research subject. Moreover as we will see, Google Scholar offers the possibility for a researcher to create inside Google Scholar (and from the data present in Google Scholar his profile).

Before using Google Scholar and to get the best possibilities offer, you should register in Google. This is free and you will need only to indicate your email and provide a password. To get register in Google you must open Google and click to CONNEXION. You will get the following screen, and click on create your account (here in French) at the bottom. During this process you will be able to put your picture, etc.

Figure 5 : Create your account

When this will be done you will get the following screen when you will open Google (either from Internet explorer or from Chrome).

Figure 6 : When toy will be registered

To go to Google Scholar, click on the square dots just after images. You will go through different screens until you reach Google Scholar.

Figure 7 : Google Scholar

When you are registered in Google, you have the facility to develop your "profile" which will appear under the heading of "My citations" (second d top right in figure 6). For the first time, to create your profile, click on my citations and follow the instructions. If you need help you may consult the power point of Dr Cheung and Leung[3]. You will have to indicate your name, email, name of your institution, etc. When your prod=file will be created, clicking on my profile, will allow you to "see" your profile and to modifier (add, or retrieve) all your papers. They can be sorted by dates or citations number. In the following figure you will see the profile of "Dou Henri" with all the papers sorted by decreasing years.

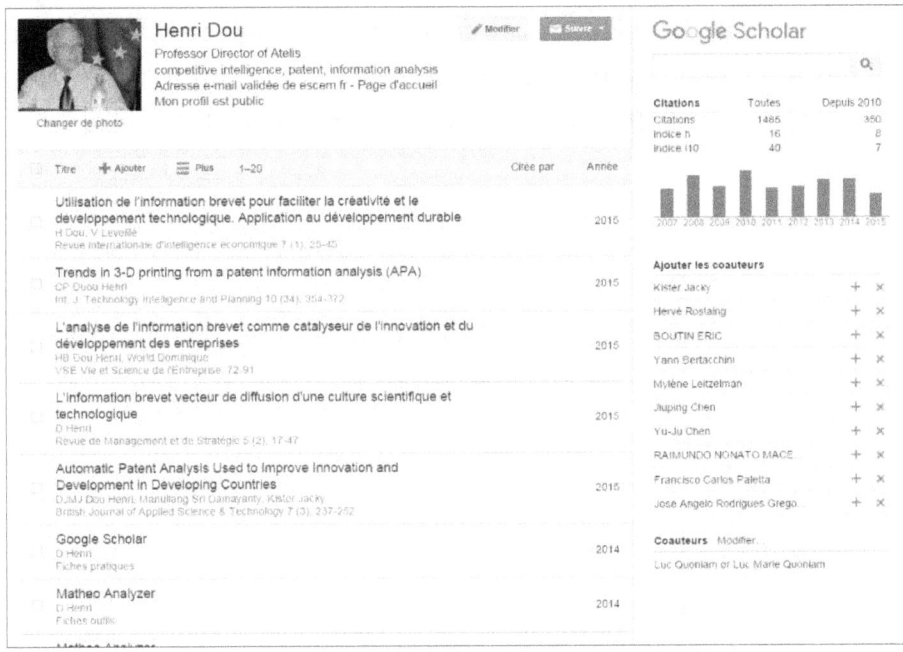

Figure 8 : My citations in Google Scholar

The left part of the screen displays your papers. You may add papers if they are not indicated, retrieve some of them if they

_____

[3] How to create your own Google Scholar Profile, http://www.ciworldwide.org

are not from you or are in duplicate, or eventually joint them is there are some misspelling so that the citations from the two papers will be added in the remaining one.

The right part of the screen display "your citations" profile per year(according the Google determination). On the left part of the screen your papers are display with their citation number. Clicking on the citation number, will display all the papers which cite your selected paper. Mind self- citations are also indicated. Then, do not abuse of them, because some people look to them and draw some conclusion about your behavior!

Using Google Scholar

As Google, Google Scholar functions in advanced mode. You move to this mode by clicking on the arrow after the search window on its left. The following figure presents it.

Figure 9 : Google Scholar in advanced mode

You may search with words, but also by author names. Here there is a search on author Dou Henri, for articles published from 2015. The result is the following.

Figure 10 : Results from the search: Dou Henri, 2015

Some features are very interesting: on top appears the profile of Dou Henri, this is the way to search for author's profile (if they create it). Most of the researchers do it and we advise you to do it if it is not already done. This will give you the same as in "my citations" for the query of the author, but you will not be able to modify his profile. Now on the left, you can modify the interval of dates for the search. On the right you can see for the last reference **[PDF] from revue-rms.fr** this indicates that this article is available in pdf format, generally free. To get the full text click on [PDF] from revue-rms.fr. Now, one of the best features of Google Scholar is to get either the related articles and even more important various citation formats for this reference for instance:

Cite

Copy and paste a formatted citation or use one of the links to import into a bibliography manager.

MLA Henri, Dou, et al. "Automatic Patent Analysis Used to Improve Innovation and Development in Developing Countries." *British Journal of Applied Science & Technology* 7.3 (2015): 237.

APA Henri, D., Damayanty, M. S., Jacky, K., & Jean-Marie Jr, D. (2015). Automatic Patent Analysis Used to Improve Innovation and Development in Developing Countries. *British Journal of Applied Science & Technology, 7*(3), 237.

Chicago Henri, Dou, Manullang Sri Damayanty, Kister Jacky, and Dou Jean-Marie Jr. "Automatic Patent Analysis Used to Improve Innovation and Development in Developing Countries." *British Journal of Applied Science & Technology* 7, no. 3 (2015): 237.

BibTeX EndNote RefMan RefWorks

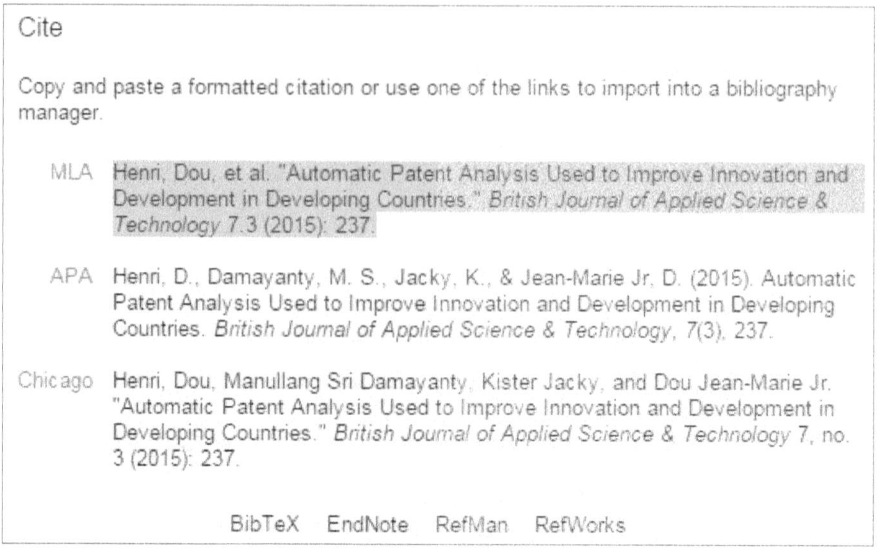

Figure 11 : Citation formats of the second article

Those formats may even be stored in various citation's management software. When you know of tedious it is to put citations in the right format when you write an article realize of it is useful!

One interesting way to use Google Scholar or Google, is to build some alerts. Google offers the facility to develop a search and when this is correct to build an alert. Which means that every time that a related information will appear in Google Scholar or in Google, the information will be sent on your email. (e-mail asked when you build the alert). Because the number items retrieve may be large, it is a good advice to create an email only affected to the alerts.

The number of information available for analysis in Google Scholar is 1000. This limits is used in PoP[4] (Publish or Perish) is used in the analysis provided by this system. The presentation will be done in the clustering engine part of this book.

[4] Harzing.com, Publish or Perish, http://www.harzing.com/resources/publish-or-perish

3 - Google Patent

Another database from Google is the database of the US patents. This database contains all the US patents, gives access to the first page or the full text and also to the drawings. All the text of the patent is indexed. This introduces sometimes some noise, because of the large numbers of words indexed. The following figure gives an example of the Google Patents retrieval. As usual an advanced mode is available. This mode will have search fields appropriate to patent searches.

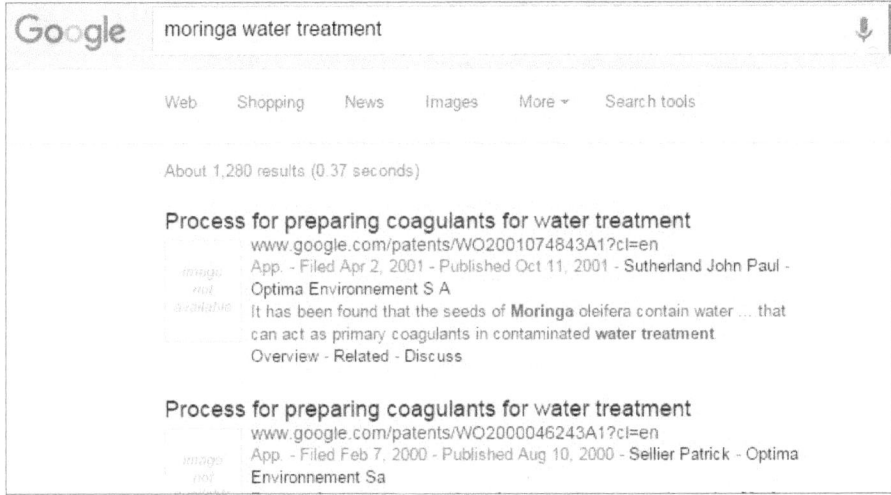

Figure 12 ; Results from Google Patent

If you click on the title of the patent, you will have the full text display as in the following figure.

Process for preparing coagulants for water treatment

WO 2001074843 A1

ABSTRACT

This invention relates to a process for preparing proteins that can act as effective coagulants in the treatment and purification of contaminated water. In particular the invention relates to a process for extracting coagulant protein derivatives from the seeds of trees from the family Moringaceae. The invention also relates to coagulation protein preparations prepared by the process, and the use of such preparations for the treatment and purification of contaminated water.

Publication number	WO2001074843 A1
Publication type	Application
Application number	PCT/GB2001/001494
Publication date	Oct 11, 2001
Filing date	Apr 2, 2001
Priority date ⓘ	Mar 31, 2000
Also published as	CN1257185C, CN1432021A, EP1268515A1, US6890565, US20020192315
Inventors	Sutherland John Paul
Applicant	Optima Environnement S A, Sutherland John Paul
Export Citation	BiBTeX, EndNote, RefMan
Patent Citations (1), Non-Patent Citations (2), Referenced by (1), Classifications (11), Legal Events (11)	
External Links: Patentscope, Espacenet	

DESCRIPTION

PROCESS FOR PREPARING COAGULANTS FOR WATER TREATMENT

The present invention relates to a process for preparing proteins that can act as effective primary coagulants in the treatment and purification of contaminated water. In particular it relates to a process for extracting coagulant protein derivatives from seeds of trees within the family Moringaceae and especially those of Moringa oleifera Lam (syns Moringa pterygosperma Gaertn.)

The seeds of Moringa oleifera Lam (hereinafter referred to as Moringa) are utilised primarily to obtain an edible oil, which is extracted using a mechanical press. The

CLAIMS (1)

1.   CLAIMS

1. A process for preparing coagulant proteins from seeds of trees of the family Moringaceae which process comprises the steps of: treating seed presscake and/or whole seed to produce and evenly divided granular powder; adding the granular powder to a complex salt solution to leach protein out of the powder; separating the protein solution from the

Figure 13 ; Full data from Google Patent

4 - Google image

This is another feature which is interesting. You must know, that it is better and faster to select somethings when you "see" it. We are going to use Google this way. Let us say that if you want to illustrate an article with the best explicit drawing using the image access is the best. For instance let us see how to illustrate the concept "Porter's 5 forces". Just make the query with "porter five forces" and select the convenient **images**.

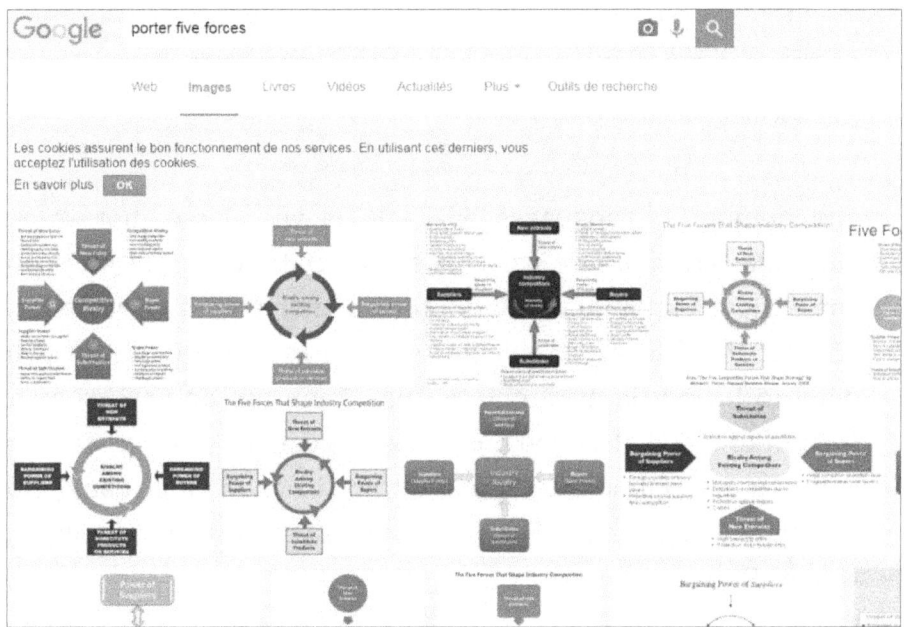

Figure 14 ; Images from "porter five forces"

Now, select the image you like and clicking on it go the corresponding URL.

5 - Google Translate

This is also a powerful facility from Google. To get Google Translate, when Google is opened, click on the square dots on the upper right. You will have a screen with various displays, and select Translate. The following figure shows a translation from Indonesian to French.

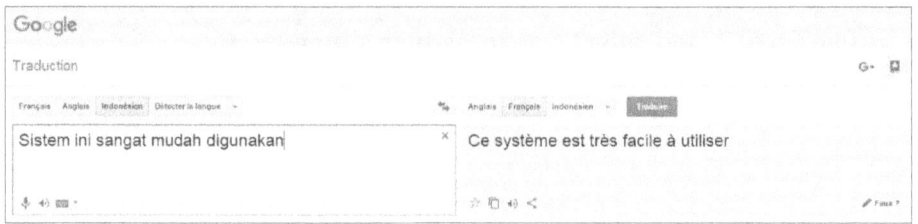

Figure 15 ; Google Translate

The number of languages available is very large, but some languages are more or less easy to translate, then you must do some tries. A little tip which is interesting. In patent for instance, you get the full text in pdf (image format). To translate it you need to have it in electronic format. Then use an OCR, submit the pdf to it and after you might use the cut and paste system to get your translation. But, if you do not have an OCR ready? Do not mind Google may afford it for free this is the next example: Google Drive.

6 - Google Drive

To get to Google Drive, when Google is opened, click on the square dot on the upper right, on select on the displays, **Drive**. To use Google Drive you need to be registered in Google.

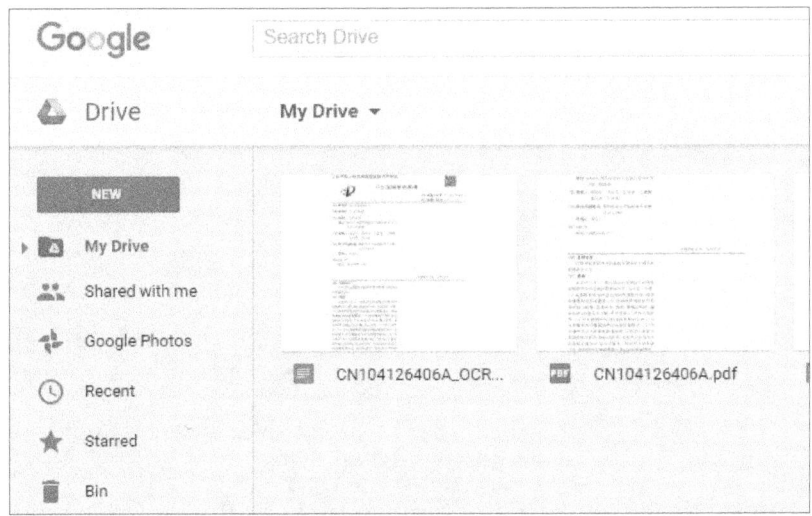

Figure 16 ; Google Drive

Her you have in Drive the text of one Chinese patent

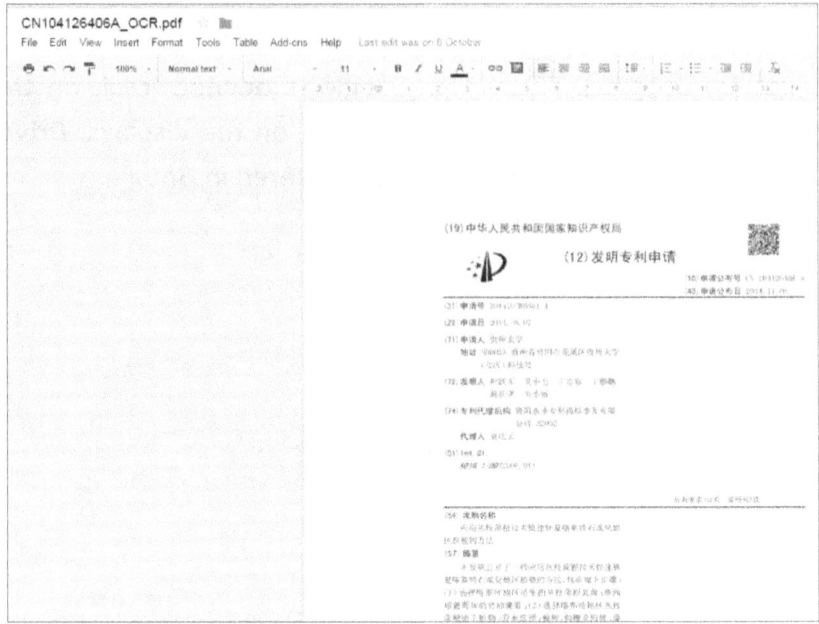

Figure 17 : Chine patent uploaded in Drive has pdf, and submits automatically to OCR in Drive

To automatically convert a pdf image to an OCRed in Drive, you must activate an option. To do it refers to the following figure[5].

---

[5] Rebecca Tarnopol, How to OCR documents for free in Google Drive, http://computers.tutsplus.com/tutorials/how-to-ocr-documents-for-free-in-google-drive--cms-20460

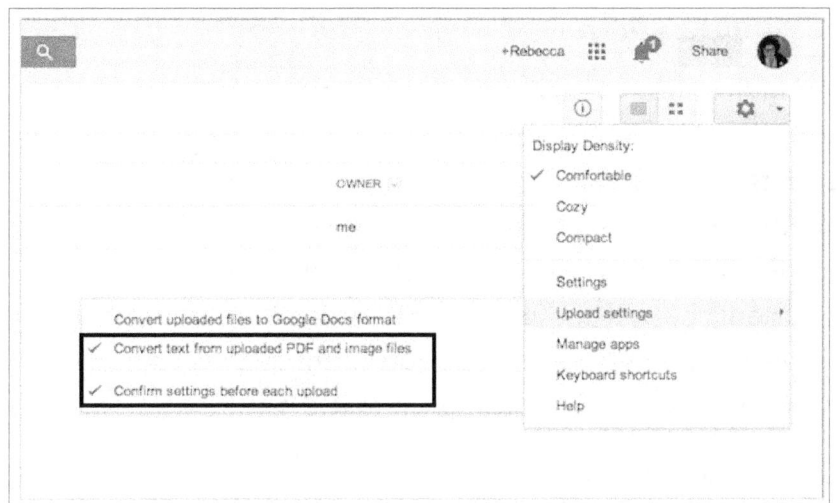

Figure 18 : Option to OCRed documents in Drive

To upload a document in Drive, click on NEW (in RED in figure 14). Drive will also allow you to share a document with other people (you will have to indicate them to Drive), and to modified the document a have it instantly available to others. (use the **Shared with me** on the right part of the screen of Drive.

7 - Google Earth

During the mast twenty years the information supports change a lot. If at the beginning it was only paper, they move to electronic formats and remain this way until now. But, the type of information is becoming more diversified: written, images, videos, etc. Among the systems available one, Google Earth is important, even if the pictures of the land are not up to date Google Earth can be used as a good information source. Here are two examples showing the interest to use it.

- A port authority in France, liked to make a study on the various facilities offered by some competitors. To benchmark the different pears and harbor basins they perform the study using Google Earth.
- A company making some fruits transformation wished to know which type of waste treatments were used by its competitors (situated far away in other countries) because that can affect the price. They know exactly their addresses, and they use in first step Google Earth to have a rough idea of the problem. Waste treatment involves settling tanks and the often voluminous works. In the following figure there is an example of one of the company analyze for waste treatment through Google Earth. The waste treatments are the facilities on the right part of the picture.

Figure 19 : Evaluation of the type of waste treatment size

8 - The videos – Youtube

If during many years the format of information has been to write articles or reports etc. or make Powerpoints ... today the number of formats which will "transport" a valuable information increase. We add first the image, then the audio, and now, the video. This is very interesting, since top people in some fields release short videos which in a few minutes will deliver the best message about the subject. Of course this is not going very deep, since the time is short, but the essential is present. So, when something new will hit you, looking for some videos on the subject is a very good practice. What may be done is to go to Google or Google Scholar for instance and detect one of the best authors in that field, and after look to see if he delivered some videos.

A good example is for instance the concept of "soft power" very important in Competitive Intelligence. It is easy to see that Joseph Nye[6] is one of the best people in that field and now if you look to Youtube and search for "soft power" and "Nye" you will get several meaningful videos[7].

---

[6] The first reference obtained with the query "soft power" is the following: Soft power - Wikipedia, the free encyclopedia https://en.wikipedia.org/wiki/**Soft_power** **Soft power** is a concept developed by **Joseph Nye** of Harvard University to describe the ability to attract and co-opt rather than coerce, use force or give money as a means of persuasion.

[7] https://www.youtube.com/watch?v=cH9hn3_Q4qQ For a short and powerful video on soft power

youtube soft power nye

Web   Videos   News   Shopping   Images   More ▾   Search tools

About 135,000 results (0.37 seconds)

Joseph Nye: Soft Power and Public Diplomacy in ... - YouTube

https://www.**youtube**.com/watch?v=DNIxR6hGAHw
Jun 23, 2011 - Uploaded by British Council
On 20 January 2010, the first anniversary of President Obamas
inauguration, US political theorist Joseph **Nye** ...

Joseph Nye on Soft Power - YouTube

https://www.**youtube**.com/watch?v=F8udhM8QKxg
Mar 12, 2009 - Uploaded by Harvard Kennedy School
Harvard Kennedy School's Joseph **Nye** is university distinguished
service professor and Sultan of Oman ...

Nye: Soft Power, Hard Power and Smart Power - YouTube

https://www.**youtube**.com/watch?v=cH9hn3_Q4qQ
Feb 29, 2012 - Uploaded by knoowii
Professor Joseph **Nye** from the Harvard Kennedy School of
Government speaks to Knoowii TV about the use ...

Joseph Nye: Soft Power and Public Diplomacy in ... - YouTube

https://www.**youtube**.com/watch?v=BBBzF631xYl
May 10, 2011 - Uploaded by British Council
On the first anniversary of President Obamas inauguration, US
political theorist Joseph **Nye** gave a lecture at ...

Figure 20 : The soft power by Joseph Nye

9 - Extracting the sound from a video coming from Youtube

Often, a video is useful not really by its images but by the sound, for instance the presentation of a topic by an expert. Then extracting the sound from the video will give you the best of the presentation within a file of a smaller size, useful to put in demo or in smartphones, etc. To do so there are two methods:

9.1 Copy the URL address of the video and open the URL http://www.youtube-mp3.org when this is done paste the URL address in the window and let the program go.

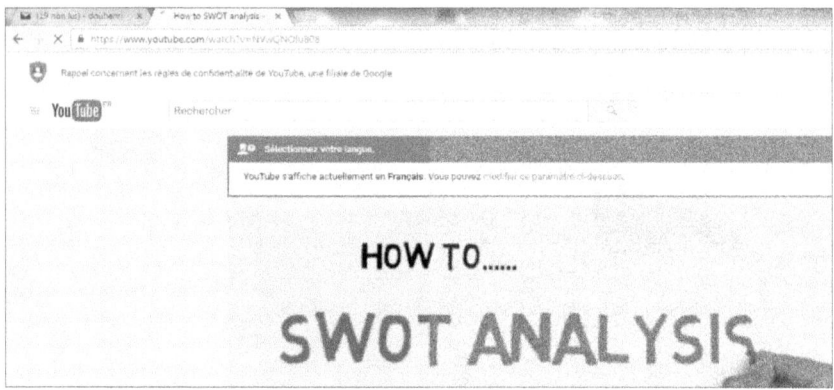

Figure 21 : Example SWOT Analysis presentation in Youtube

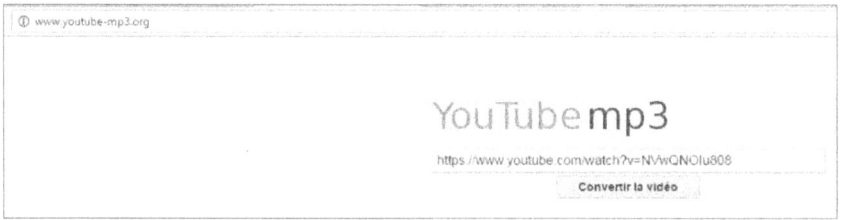

Figure 22 : Youtube mp3

9.2 Sometimes a message from Youtube indicates that there is an error or that the sound cannot be extracted. In this case use the second method, in the url of the video copy the word SON just before Youtube and go. After follow the instructions, this will drive you to another host and the sound will be extracted.

Figure 23 : SonYoutube

10 - The bookmark

The bookmark is very useful and may be used in various ways: to store the addresses of various Internet sites, to store Internet pages addresses (for instance the address of a full text article, or the different profiles of authors, etc.). You will have 45 characters to name the address leading to unless using the automatic naming of it. All the addresses can be store in your bookmark in different folders, opening wide possibilities. For instances on a database of IPC (Internet Patent Classification) you must select the addresses of the classes the most important for you and save their addresses under a special folder. This will save time to get them without going through the database and selecting the class. An example will be given when we will present the Patent Databases. The data in your bookmarks may be modified or deleted as you decide.

Your book mark may also be exchanged with other people. it is interesting if you have to work for instance in on a search involving the consultation of various Internet site pages. Exchanging you bookmark with somebody working on the same subject will save a lot of time and writing. Exchanging Bookmark can be done by using various bookmarking sites[8] such as delicious[9] for instance. These sites allow you to exchange your bookmark with other people. Il you want to exchange your bookmark with some safety and do not get them public, the best is to copy the folder FAVORIS (Bookmarks or else in another language) which is located in (for PC and with Internet Explorer)

---

[8] Social Benchmarking Sites, http://www.searchenginejournal.com/50-social-bookmarking-sites-importance-of-user-generated-tags-votes-and-links/6066/

[9] Delicious Website, https://en.wikipedia.org/wiki/Delicious_(website)

drive **C:** then **Utilisateur** then **Utilisateur** then folder **Favoris** (User, User, bookmarks in English) The other people will have just to put it at the same place on his computer. This is the way to consult your bookmark with Internet Explorer. For the users of Chrome you will have to transfer your bookmark from Internet explorer to Chrome. You will do it this way when Chrome is open.

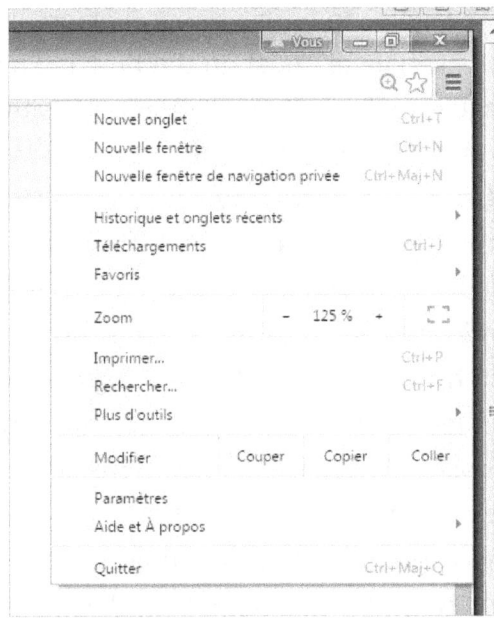

Figure 24 : Transferring you Bookmark to Chrome (top right)

Choose "Favoris" (Bookmarks or else in other languages) this will open a windows on which you will select "Importer les favoris et les paramètres" (import bookmarks and parameters) and after select from Internet Explorer.

11 – Languages in Google

With Google there are various ways to use languages. You may perform a query in one language for instance in French, and select the answers which will be only in English. To choose the response languages go to Google in advance mode and select the corresponding language. But, to get the best from Google, it is important to consider that the various hosts available are not all in the same language. One of the classical errors is to perform a query only in one language (most on the time in English or worse only in the language of your country) and consider that this is sufficient. This is not true. When you query the Web, you must consider and this is an expertise by itself, in which language you expect to get the best set of answers. If for instance you intend to get information on Brazil, the best will be to make a query in Portuguese and also in English. If you do not know the Portuguese, use the translate facility in Google. The answers will be for most of them in the same language, but note that Google proposes for most of the answers the translation. If this is not the case, use again Google translate. The importance of languages in the Web underlines their importance in Competitive Intelligence. Today, the development of China, India, Indonesia provides millions of data in different languages that the Western ones. This increases the complexity compare to the situation 10 years ago where English was sufficient. Today, depending of the plants of your company, the use of various languages will be necessary. Another point which is important when you use a translator: all the time it uses a pivot language which is English. (to go from Indonesian to French, the translator goes first to English and after from English to French) Then to get the best possible translation translate in English that will be more relevant.

12 - Conclusion

The facilities offer by Google if they are used properly offer many possibilities to retrieve information, to translate it if necessary, to organize your work with co-workers even on a remote base. If you spend a little time to practice, this is also interesting than playing videos games, you will acquire rapidly the expertise and then be able to work faster and better. Do not forget that the information may come in various ways, video, e-books, articles, audio books, videos. The only problem is time, since if you want to read everything you will spend too much time and you will not have the time to do! So, the best way is to practice and to get the necessary "serendipity", and have always present, that knowledge is not found, it must be created.

Part 2 : The Clustering Engines

The clustering engines[10] are part of the Web 2.0. They use web data to extract them and treat them according various mathematical algorithms and present the results as interactive graphs. They are many types of clustering engines, some of them are free with paying options, others are available throughout subscriptions, etc. To clarify ideas we will present different examples of clustering engines available freely. They are often useful when you want to have a broad idea of a subject in a very few time, or if you wish to have nice pictures to introduce the subject of a presentation.

1 - Carrot2

Carrot2[11] is a clustering engine which deals with two different information sources. One if the Web the other Medline[12]. In this example we will deal with the concept of Moringa[13] (the miracle tree)

---

[10] Ferragina, P., & Gulli, A. (2004, November). The anatomy of a hierarchical clustering engine for Web-page, news and book snippets. In *Data Mining, 2004. ICDM'04. Fourth IEEE International Conference on* (pp. 395-398). IEEE.

[11] Osiński, S., & Weiss, D. (2005). Carrot2: Design of a flexible and efficient web information retrieval framework. In *Advances in Web Intelligence* (pp. 439-444). Springer Berlin Heidelberg.

[12] Mdeline is a database dealing with medical and biomedical scientific articles. It access is free.

[13] Moringa Oleifera from Wikipedia
https://en.wikipedia.org/wiki/Moringa_oleifera

1.1 Using the Web

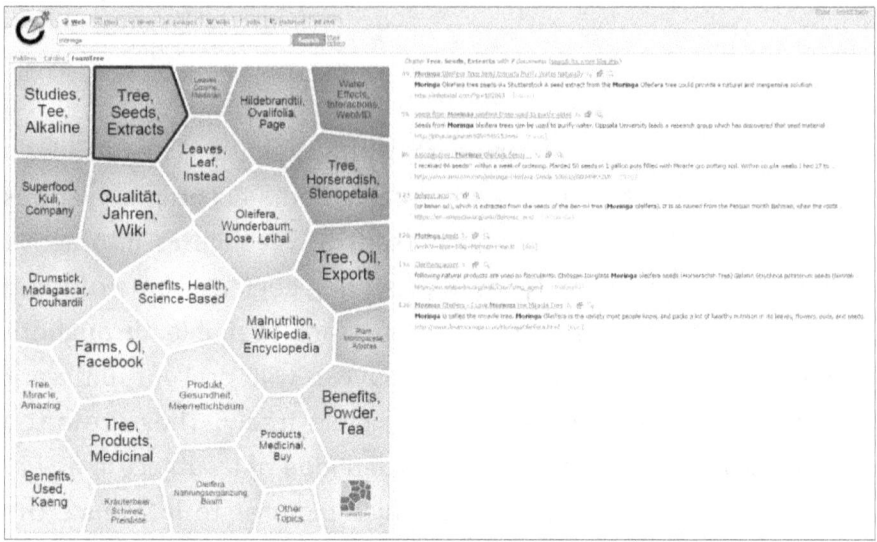

Figure 25 : Web analysis with Carrot 2, subject Moringa. Foam representation

When you select one of the foam, you have on the right the corresponding web sites. This version is free, paying options allow you to use more web data and other representations as indicated in the following figure.

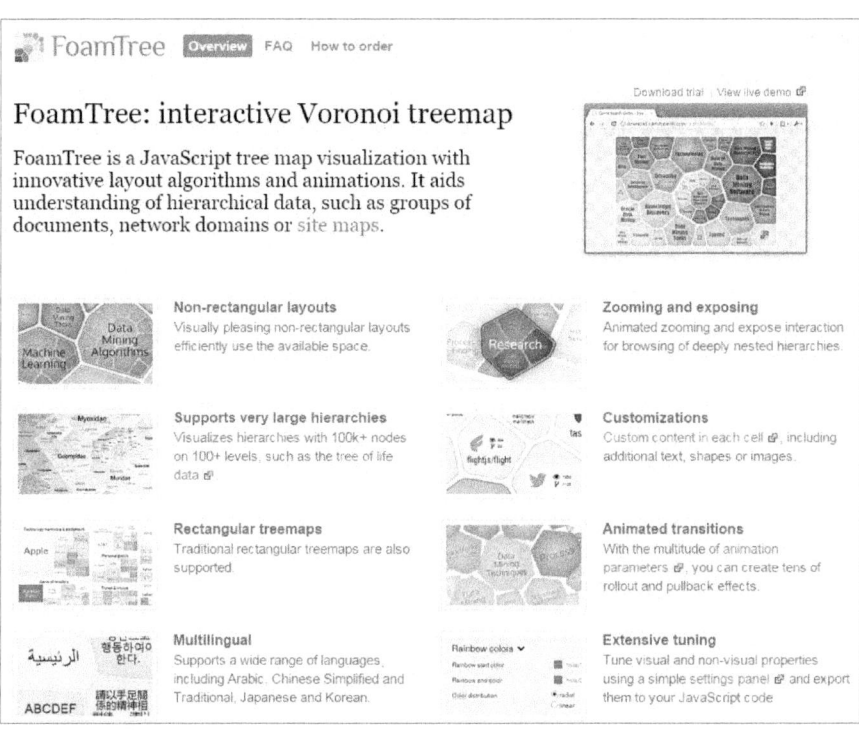

Figure 26 : Foam tree representations (Carrot2)

1.2 Using Pubmed

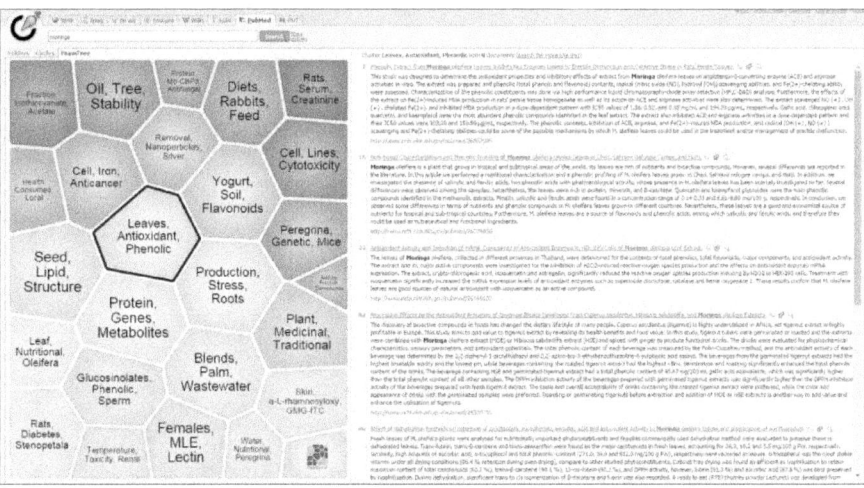

Figure 27 : Medline analysis with Carrot 2, subject Moringa. Foam representation

When you select one of the foam, the Medline references appears on the left. Clicking on the title directs you to the Medline datable to get the full bibliographic reference with the abstract.

2 - Newsmap

Newsmap[14] is a clustering engine which deals with general information from press agencies releases, etc. We use here the free limited version, you select the type of information and the clustering engine do the rest of the job.

2.1 World news

Figure 28 : Newsmap, subject selected World (bottom bar) Info in Australia (top bar)

The larger the box the more important (in number of articles it is). In the free version one information is displayed when you select the box. (here selection of Paris attacks: ....).

---

[14] http://newsmap.jp/#/n/au/view/

2.2 Technology

The selection of the domain is "technology", and the country selected "India"

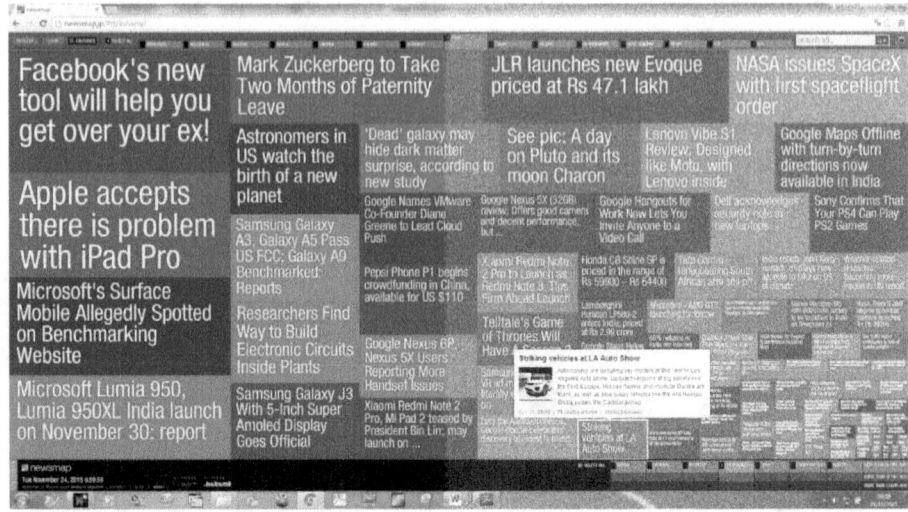

Figure 29 : The new in technology from India

3 - Using Google News

The news information may also in another format and with another selection of data, be obtained throughout the option NEWS from Google. Here is an example dealing with the search Moringa in the Google's new option.

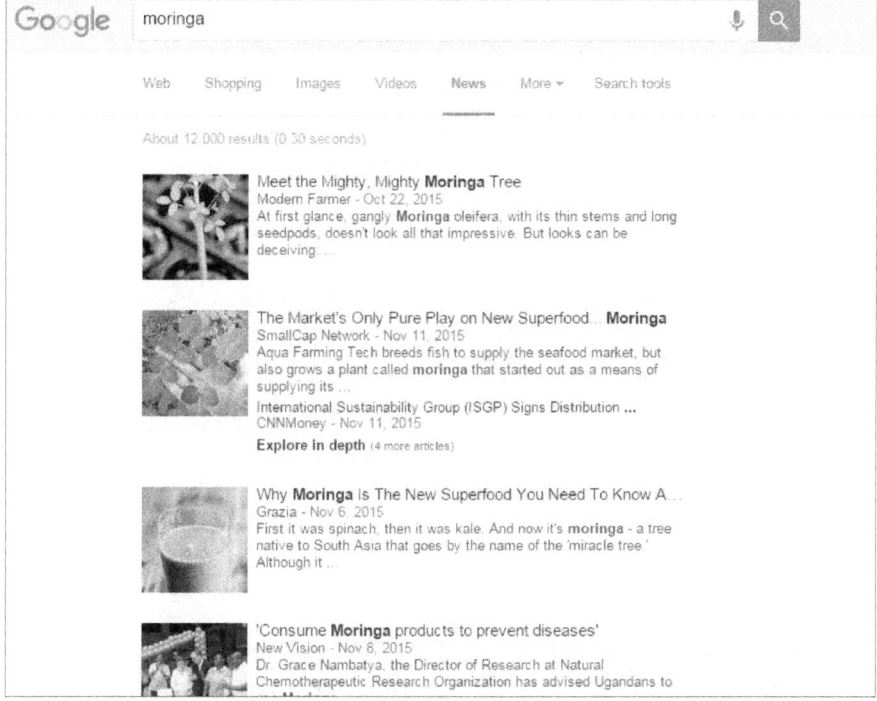

Figure 30 : Searching in Google with the NEWS option. Here Moringa

4 - iBoogie

Iboogie[15] [16] is a clustering engine which deals with various sites. In the free version the information source used is MSN. Here is in the following figure an example with Moringa (one of the best plant to struggle with malnutrition, deforestation, etc. This plant (bush) concerns mainly the African countries.

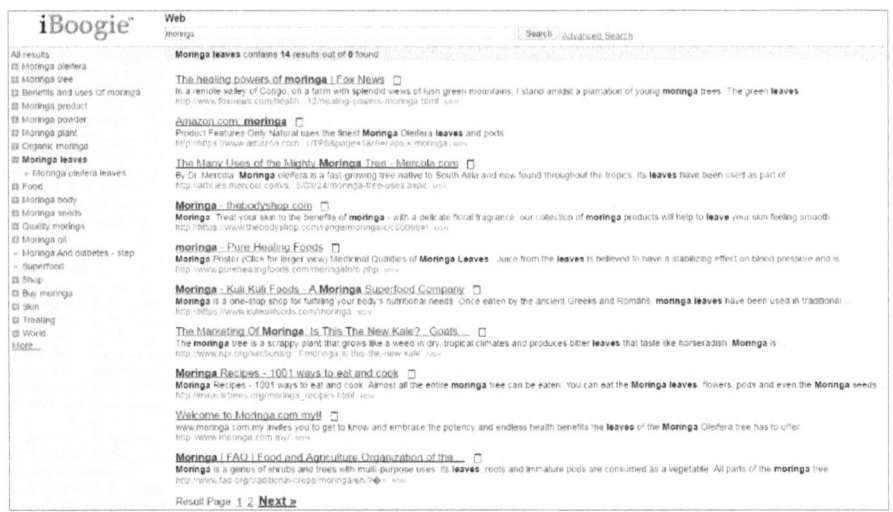

Figure 31 : iBoogie clustering engine dealing with commercial sites – Here Moringa

The data clustered data are presented on the left. Clicking on one of the data gives on the right the corresponding URL. Here we choose Moringa Leaves. Clicking on the title (right part of the screen) opens the Internet site.

---

[15]http://iboogie.com/searchtree.asp?name_news_tab=0&name_tab=0 &name_query=moringa&name_action=1&name_res_html_id=34&na me_html_id=34&tick=144761

[16] Wan, X., Gao, J., Li, M., & Ding, B. (2005, October). Person resolution in person search results: Webhawk. In *Proceedings of the 14th ACM international conference on Information and knowledge management* (pp. 163-170). ACM.

iBoogie may also be used with author names. For instance the search with dou henri" will give various results among which many will deal with homonyms or with part of the name "Henri", for "Henri Salvador" (a French singer).

The same type of search can also be done with company names.

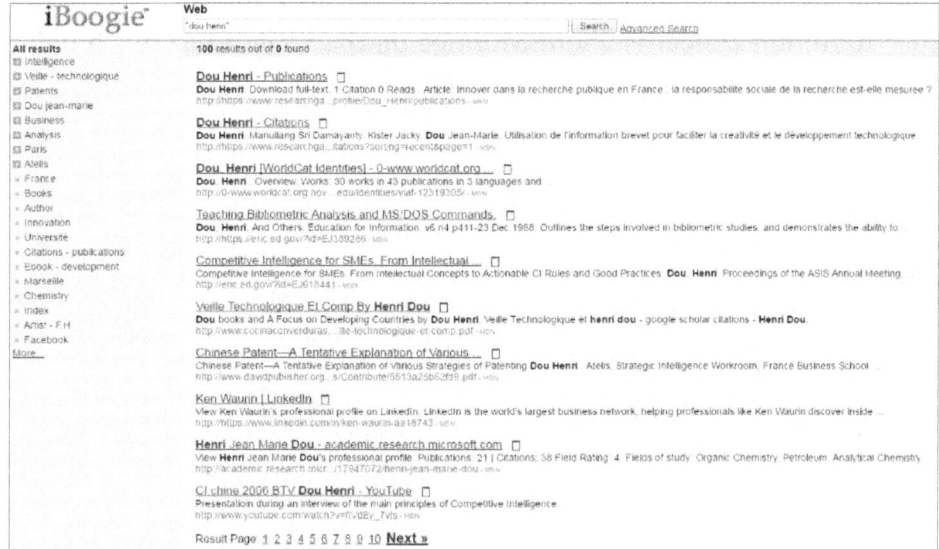

Figure 32 : iBoogie and author names (note the presence of brackets around the name)

Figure 33 : iBoogie with a Company name (here "l'occitane", a French beauty company

5 - Wikimindmap[17]

This clustering engine used as a source the various items which are described in the Wikipedia sites (English but also other languages)[18]. In the following figure we give some representation of Moringa, with the point of view of the English wiki, and also the French one. The differences between both wikis show the different concerns about Moringa on the English or French point of view.

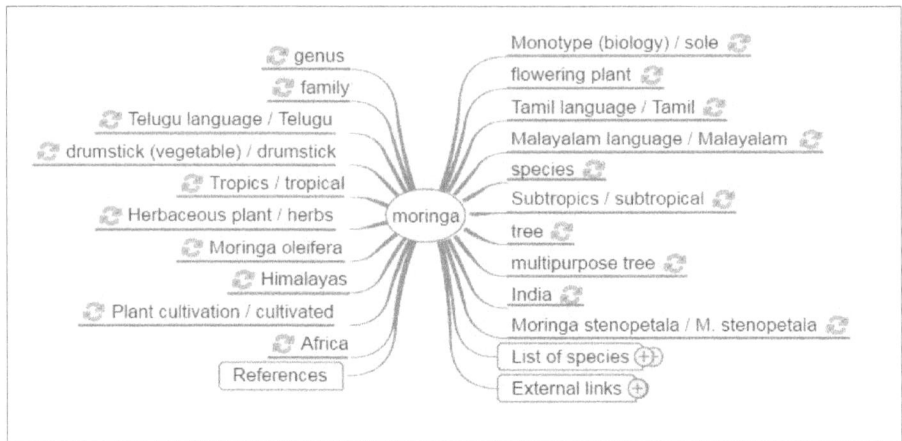

Figure 34 : English Wiki used with Moringa

The + sign indicates that clicking on it will open more wiki descriptions and links.

---

[17] http://www.wikimindmap.org/

[18] Laika's MedLibLog, WikiMindMap to Organize Wiki Content

https://laikaspoetnik.wordpress.com/2008/08/17/wikimindmap-to-organize-wiki-content/

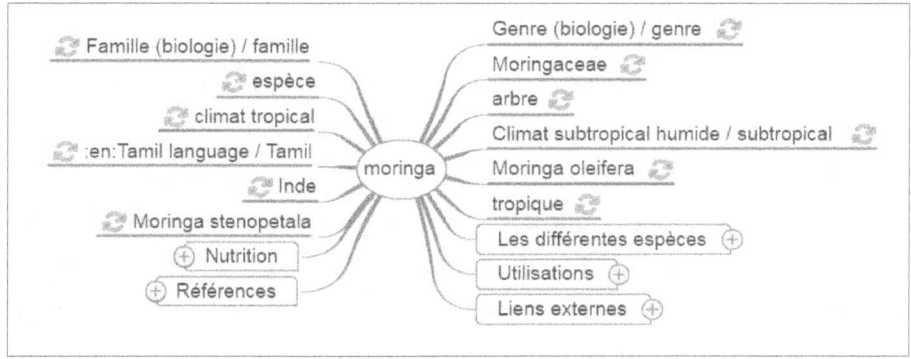

Figure 35 : French Wiki used with Moringa

Note the differences, mainly with the appearance of Nutrition+ and Utilisations+. These rubrics indicate a stronger concern of Moringa in the French community, which can be easily understood because of the French Community in Africa.

6 - Euristic maps

They are representations of various results from different information sources queries. For instance wikimindmap[19] allows you to represent the data from Wikipedia's queries. Other euristic maps are available through the mind mapping[20] . The mind mapping has for objective to organize information and presents it on the most useful ways to help brain storming, innovation etc. We will not go further in the presentation of mind mapping since most of the time it is coming after the information retrieval. Some software do for instance with Internet both actions in the same time: search (according on or several words) and represent the information with a map of relationships[21]. One of the objectives is to connect the information to a central subject[22]. The following figure present some view of a mind mapping[23].

---

[19] Caruso, G. P., L. Ferlino, and L. Oliva. "Wikimindmap, an open Source Tool for a Comprehensive View of a Wikipedia Item."*Edulearn12 Proceedings* (2012): 4620-4629.
[20] Frey, Chuck. "Mind Mapping Software User Survey." *Mind Mapping Software Blog* (2010).
[21] https://en.wikipedia.org/wiki/Mind_map
[22] http://lifehacker.com/how-to-use-mind-maps-to-unleash-your-brains-creativity-1348869811
[23] 15 common mind mapping elements
http://mindmappingsoftwareblog.com/15-common-mind-map-elements/

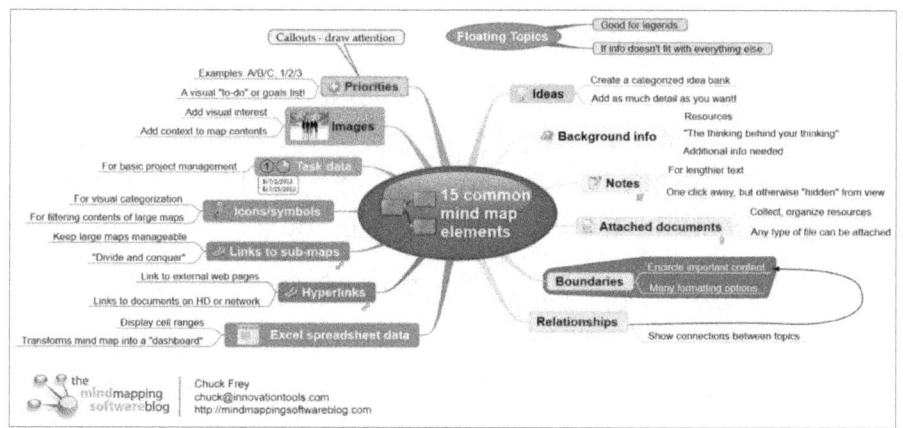

Figure 36 : Mind mapping (Example)

If long time ago people use a paper board to draw mind map, today software allows to make it, some of them facilitate the drawing only, others, the most interesting allow to link information (web site addresses, spread sheets, data, word files, ppt, etc...) to each of the ideas presents on the map. This is important because it substitutes facts to feelings.

7 - Other representations

There are many ways to represent information. We will just present in the following figure the representation of a text through an analysis if its content and highlighting the most important words. This is the case of TagCrowd[24]

Here is a text[25] about Moringa:

In Western countries, dried leaves are sold as dietary supplements, in either powder or capsule form. Compared to the leaves, the pods are generally lower in vitamins and minerals. However, they are exceptionally rich in vitamin C. One cup of fresh, sliced pods (100 grams) contains 157% of your daily requirement for vitamin C (3). The diets of people in developing nations sometimes lack vitamins, minerals and protein. In these countries, Moringa oleifera can be an important source of many essential nutrients. However, there is one downside. Moringa leaves may also contain high levels of antinutrients, which can reduce the absorption of minerals and protein (4, 5). Another thing to keep in mind is that if you're taking Moringa oleifera as a supplement, taking it in capsules won't supply large amounts of nutrients. The amounts are negligible compared to what you are already getting if you eat a balanced, real food-based diet.

Here is its representation in TagCrowd

24 http://tagcrowd.com/
25 http://authoritynutrition.com/6-benefits-of-moringa-oleifera/

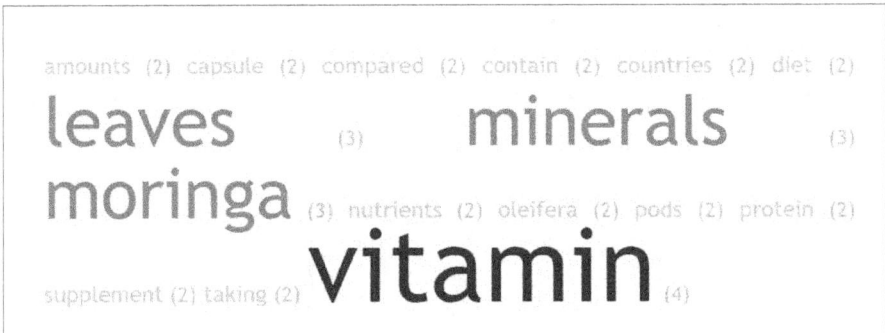

amounts (2) capsule (2) compared (2) contain (2) countries (2) diet (2)
leaves (3) minerals (3)
moringa (3) nutrients (2) oleifera (2) pods (2) protein (2)
vitamin (4)
supplement (2) taking (2)

Figure 37 : Text representation with TagCrowd

It is also possible to analyze a web page and to fix the number of words to be visualized.

8 – Kartoo a pre-defined search engine

Kartoo[26] is a meta search engine which works on pre-defined information domains.

Figure 38 : Query interface from Kartoo

Let us for instance choose the Computer, High-Tech domain (you click on the name).

---

[26] http://uk.kartoo.com/

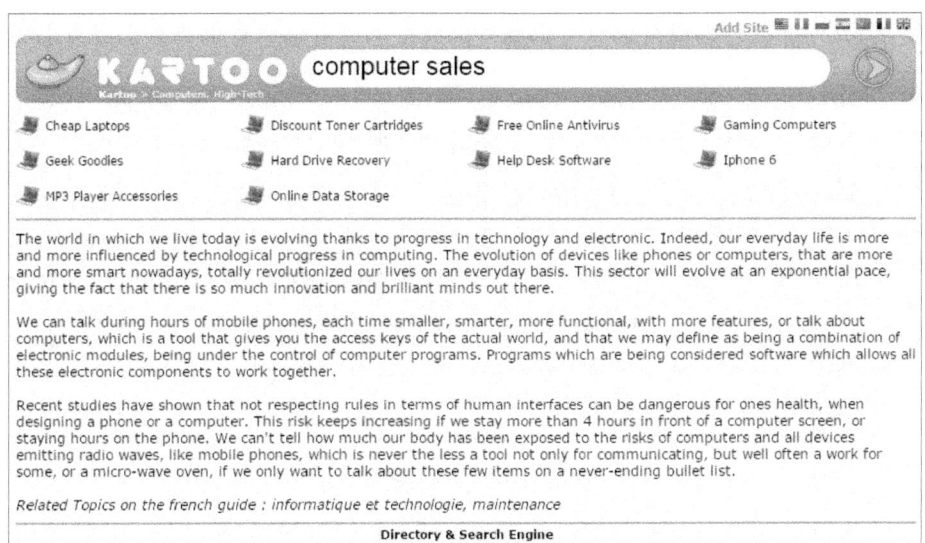

KARTOO | computer sales ▶

Kartoo > Computers, High-Tech

Cheap Laptops	Discount Toner Cartridges	Free Online Antivirus	Gaming Computers
Geek Goodies	Hard Drive Recovery	Help Desk Software	Iphone 6
MP3 Player Accessories	Online Data Storage		

The world in which we live today is evolving thanks to progress in technology and electronic. Indeed, our everyday life is more and more influenced by technological progress in computing. The evolution of devices like phones or computers, that are more and more smart nowadays, totally revolutionized our lives on an everyday basis. This sector will evolve at an exponential pace, giving the fact that there is so much innovation and brilliant minds out there.

We can talk during hours of mobile phones, each time smaller, smarter, more functional, with more features, or talk about computers, which is a tool that gives you the access keys of the actual world, and that we may define as being a combination of electronic modules, being under the control of computer programs. Programs which are being considered software which allows all these electronic components to work together.

Recent studies have shown that not respecting rules in terms of human interfaces can be dangerous for ones health, when designing a phone or a computer. This risk keeps increasing if we stay more than 4 hours in front of a computer screen, or staying hours on the phone. We can't tell how much our body has been exposed to the risks of computers and all devices emitting radio waves, like mobile phones, which is never the less a tool not only for communicating, but well often a work for some, or a micro-wave oven, if we only want to talk about these few items on a never-ending bullet list.

Related Topics on the french guide : informatique et technologie, maintenance

Directory & Search Engine

Figure 39 : Using Kartoo

You may now, choose a specific domain and obtain information about it.

9 - Conclusion

They are many ways to represent information. What you must keep in mind, is that some people are more receptive to reading, others to visual representations and the representation becomes tool to communicate. When you want very rapidly to have an idea of "what is going on" on a specific point, it takes just a few minutes to use a clustering engine and get a right vision of it. Most of the times we use Carrot: it gives good results and the nice colored pictures.

Often, if you are engaged in Competitive Intelligence or in think tanks or in strategic groups you will participate to brain storming. One way to make the brain storming efficient is to use the appropriate software[27] to link ideas but also to associate automatically these ideas with true information. This is the best way to build mind maps.

---

[27] Essential mind mapping and brain storming tools
http://mashable.com/2013/09/25/mind-mapping-tools/#1G2vN8rTaGqh

Index of figures